# Basic Defense & Safety Fundamentals for Pool & Pocket Billiards

How to make smart game decisions

Allan P. Sand,

PBIA Certified Instructor

ISBN: 978-1-62505-004-5
Print 7x10

ISBN 978-1-62505-377-0
Print 6x9

ISBN 978-1-62505-535-4
eBook format

First edition

Copyright © 2015 Allan P. Sand

All rights reserved under International and Pan-American Copyright Conventions.

Published by Billiard Gods Productions.

Santa Clara, CA 95051

U.S.A.

For the latest information about books and videos, go to:
http://www.billiardgods.com

**Acknowledgements**

Wei Chao created the software that was used to create these graphics.

*Basic Defense & Safety Fundamentals*

## Table of Contents

**Introduction** ............................................................................... 1
**Types of Safeties** ..................................................................... 2
Bad Angle Safety Type ................................................................. 2
Distance Safety Type .................................................................... 3
Frozen Cushion Safety Type ........................................................ 4
Hidden Ball Safety Type ............................................................... 5
**Safety Exercises** ..................................................................... 8
Cue Ball Speed Control ................................................................ 8
Cue Ball Position Control ............................................................. 9
Object Ball Position Control ....................................................... 11
Cue Ball Follow Control .............................................................. 12
Cue Ball Stun Control ................................................................. 14
Cue Ball Draw Control ................................................................ 15
**Safety Basics** ......................................................................... 16
Know Your Comfort/Chaos Zones ............................................. 16
Recognizing Opponent's Bad Habits ........................................ 17
Dead Zones ................................................................................. 21
Dangers of "Ball-in-Hand" ......................................................... 23
Stupid Hero (& Superhero) Shots ............................................. 24
Ensuring Insurance Balls ........................................................... 24
    *8 Ball Insurance* ............................................................... *25*
    *9 Ball Insurance* ............................................................... *25*
How to Win Safety Battles ......................................................... 26
    *8 Ball Safety Battle Tips* ................................................... *26*
    *9 Ball Safety Battle Tips* ................................................... *27*
How to Make Safety Mistakes ................................................... 27
How to Learn from Playing Errors ............................................. 28
How to Select the Best Shot ...................................................... 29
Hidden Ball Shadows ................................................................. 31
**Safety Tactics** ........................................................................ 34
Tactical Options & Choices ........................................................ 34
Smart Missing ............................................................................. 35
    *8 Ball Smart Miss* ............................................................. *35*
    *9 Ball Smart Miss* ............................................................. *36*
Bank into a Safety ...................................................................... 38
Creating Pocket Blockers ........................................................... 39
Figuring BPI (balls per inning) Average .................................... 40
End-game Tactics ....................................................................... 42
Use Hangers as Traps ................................................................ 42
How to Shoot Two-Way Shots ................................................... 43

**Miscellaneous ................................................................. 46**
The "Ownership" Test ............................................................... 46
How to Escape a Hidden Ball Safety Against You ........................... 47
How to Calculate One Cushion Kicks ............................................ 48
How to Make Two Cushion Kicks .................................................. 49
A Recommended Basic Practice Routine ....................................... 50
Random Ball Practicing .............................................................. 50
8 Ball Offense-Defense Game ..................................................... 50
9 Ball Offense-Defense Game ..................................................... 51
Chase - a Game to Learn Kicking Skills ........................................ 51


## By the author …

Why Pool Hustlers Win

Table Map Library

Safety Toolbox

Cue Ball Control Cheat Sheets

Advanced Cue Ball Control Self-Testing Program

Drills & Exercises for Pool & Pocket Billiards

The Art of War versus The Art of Pool

3 Cushion Billiards Championship Shots (a series)

Carom Billiards: Some Riddles & Puzzles

Carom Billiards: MORE Riddles & Puzzles

The Psychology of Losing – Tricks, Traps & Sharks

The Art of Team Coaching

The Art of Personal Competition

The Art of Politics & Campaigning

The Art of Marketing & Promotion

Kitchen God's Guide for Single Guys

# Introduction

The information provided here will eventually ensure that you become a tough competitor and a dangerous player. This book presents information that will help get you past the bar-banger stage of your pool playing career. The information learned here and from the exercises will set your feet firmly upon the path of continued improvements to the intermediate level. When your defensive skills in this book become second nature, get the more advanced *Safety Toolbox*, which will further your competitive abilities.

The fundamental concepts presented in this book are when to consider defensive tactics and how to select the most effective shot. This new awareness allows you to consider the many ways to offer your opponent one of many possible unfriendly layouts. You are going to have to give up one very bad habit – letting your imagination run wild.

Let your opponent continue following the bar-banger style of calling fantastic hero shots, such as, "5 ball, four rails, off the 7 and into the side pocket." It is a sign of pool player maturity to stop playing shots that a five-year-old can recognize as dumb. With that change in your attitude, this book, and some practice sessions, you can start using a few of those brain cells to make better playing decisions.

I don't need to wish you good luck. This book and some of your time is all you need to begin winning more games. You will actually discover that you can win more games simply by preventing your opponent from winning. And it is also more fun that simply outshooting him.

# Types of Safeties

Remember this - you are not playing a professional who can take advantage of your slightest mistake and run out the table. You are competing against someone around your skill level. That means that a bad situation for you will also be a problem for your opponent.

These are the basic safety types that are easy to understand, practice, and learn to control. There are other safety types, but these are the most commonly used.

You don't need to spend hours and hours practicing, but five or ten minutes working with these different types and some of the other exercises will have very beneficial results. With just these four types (and various combinations), you can keep an opponent off-balance and under your control.

The important and useful types of safeties are:

- Bad angle – tough or impossible cut shot.
- Distance – object ball far, far away.
- Frozen cushion – force a shot off the rail.
- Hidden ball – force a kick for a legal hit.

## Bad Angle Safety Type

A bad angle is any shot that you can't make – and if you can't make it, your opponent will have the same problem. The level of difficulty for you defines the quality of trouble for your opponent.

These are easy to set up. For 8 Ball, the focus in on placing the cue ball in a position related to your opponent's object balls. For 9 Ball, your focus is more on object ball control with secondary concern on cue ball placement.

This safety type has a high tolerance factor and does not require precise control. It can easily be combined with the other safety types. When your opponent always tries to make a shot, you can entertain yourself by setting up bad angle after bad angle.

In pool, there is always a luck factor. When your opponent tries some crazy shot, the chances of failure are high, but not necessarily impossible. If the shot is somehow made, congratulate your opponent on his "billiard god luck". This will encourage him to continue attempting those same near-impossible shots. (It's always nice when your opponent helps you beat him.)

### Bad Angle Safety Type examples

Because these shots are tough for you – they are tough for your opponent.

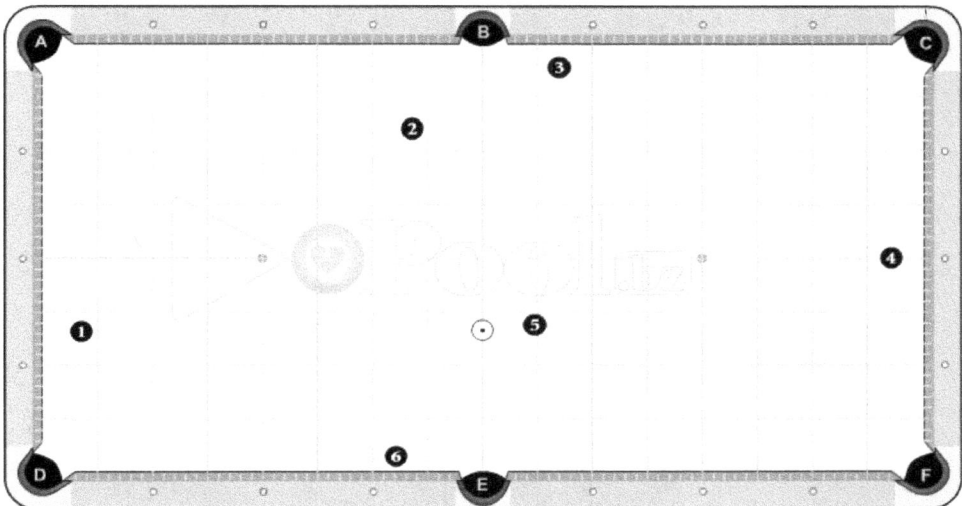

## Distance Safety Type

The distance safety type has a single purpose - give your opponent a long green shot. There can be an available pocket to make the ball, but it is the sheer distance that lowers your opponent's chances of success.

There are two kinds of distance safeties. One is when the cue ball must travel over a lot of table cloth before it contacts the object ball. The other is when the object ball must travel over a lot of table cloth to get to a pocket.

For 8 Ball, the focus is on placing the cue ball in a position away from your opponent's object balls. For 9 Ball, the focus is on object ball control with secondary concern on cue ball placement.

Your opponent might make this type of shot once in a while, but the chances of missing are to your advantage. And because he has to concentrate so hard, his ability to get position on another ball will be limited.

The distance safety type can also be combined with the bad angle safety type or the frozen cushion safety type. This makes the shot even more frustrating for an opponent who doesn't know what you know about offense and defense.

*Distance Safety Type examples*
Force your opponent to shoot an object ball into a pocket far, far away.

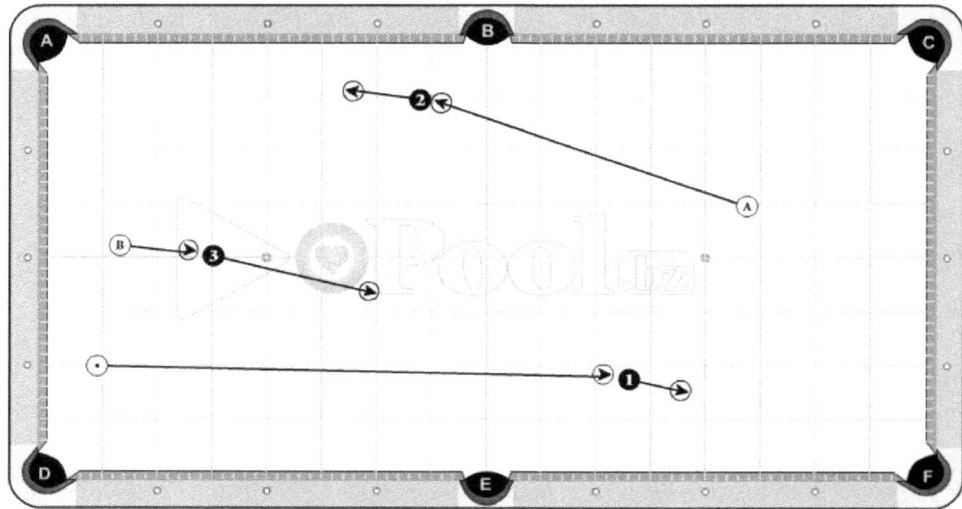

# Frozen Cushion Safety Type

A frozen cushion safety type is an evil shot – to most players. Usually, you see players jacking up the cue stick to stab down on the shot. This makes it a tough shot and is easy to miscue. Unless well-practiced, most players find this type of shot difficult to control after the stroke.

Most players hate this type of shot. It presents a lot of uncomfortable problems. An improperly chalked tip causes miscues. When the cue is jacked up to shoot down at the cue ball, all sorts of bad things can happen – miscue, unintended masse, uncomfortable stance, poor aiming, and a general desire to get the shot over with because of this discomfort. For players who exhibit this behavior, be a nice guy and provide many opportunities.

> ***How to shoot this shot:*** When you shoot a ball up against the cushion, do it correctly. Position your stick parallel to the floor and slide the stick over the

cushion to contact the upper part of the cue ball. Make sure you are well-chalked. It doesn't take much practice to make this a routine shot.

It is easy to set up this kind of safety, especially if your target object ball is close to a nearby rail. Avoid the attempt to lay a cue ball onto a rail after contacting two or three cushions. That kind of imaginative shot should be avoided.

### *How to Lay the Cue Ball on the Cushion examples*

These examples show how easy it is to set up this kind of safety type.

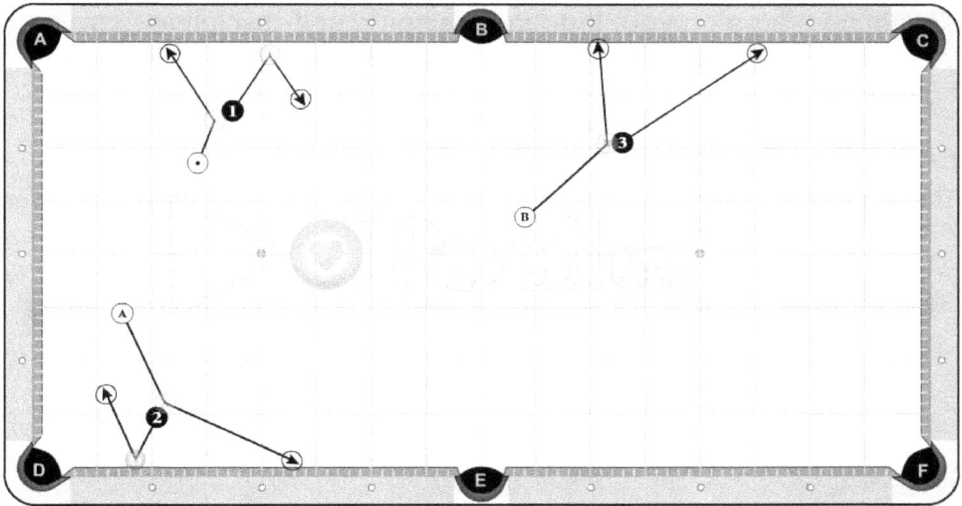

## Hidden Ball Safety Type

Most players think this is the only "real" safety. You want to encourage that false belief. This helps because your opponent will not consider shooting the other real safeties (distance, bad angle, and frozen cushion). That ignorance will help you win.

Your opportunities for a hidden ball safety will arise more often by accident. You only have to recognize the opportunity. If you are properly analyzing table layouts, you can easily identify when an easy hidden ball safety occurs.

To your benefit, the majority of your opponents are so focused on playing an offensive shot that they entirely miss an obvious and very simple hidden ball opportunity. You might say, if it was a snake, it would bite their nose and they still wouldn't see the snake.

When you observe him throwing away such an opportunity, breathe a sigh of relief.

Generally, stay away from complicated attempts to play a hidden ball safety. As soon as you dream up the idea of a precise placement of the object ball or cue ball, you had better slap yourself awake. Complicated shots almost always predictably fail. Avoid any kind of fantastical attempt will only embarrass you.

Use the KISS approach (Keep It Simple, Stupid). Allowing yourself to attempt a stupid shot is – well, stupid. Look for easy and simple solutions. It does take some effort to look for the simple solution. This is no blame on you. It does take some self-discipline to train yourself, but after some experience, you will have yourself under control.

### *Easy 8 Ball Hidden Ball Safety Type examples*

These are very simple shots and very troublesome for your opponents - once you learn how to look for them.

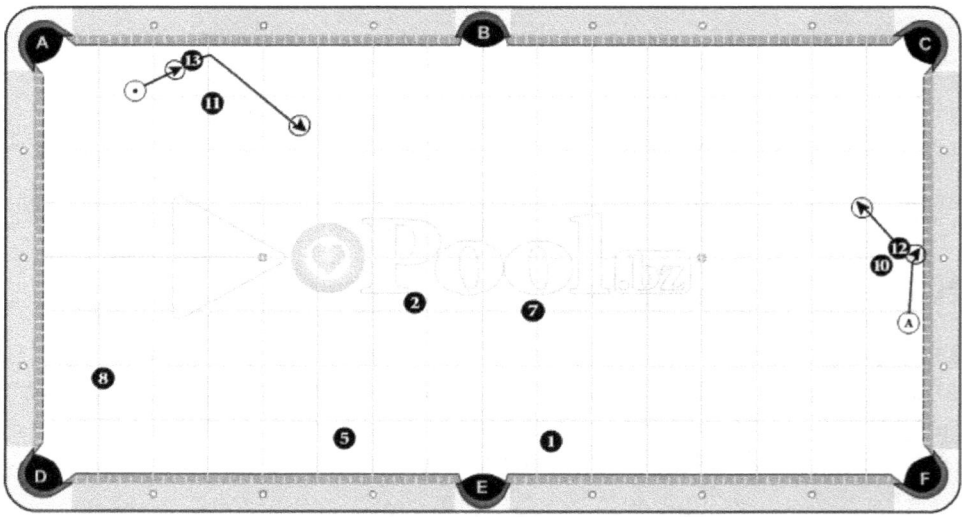

## Easy 9 Ball Hidden Ball Safety Type examples

A simple stun shot will keep the cue ball hidden.

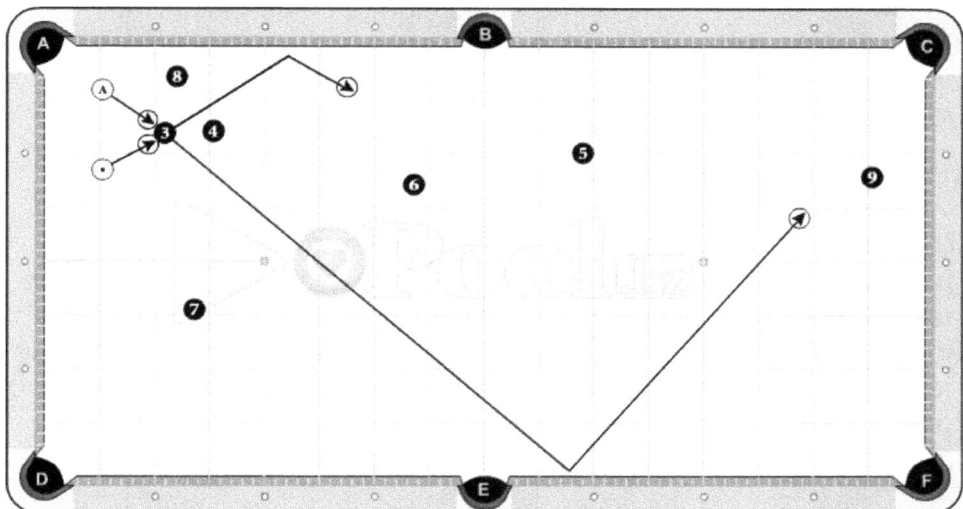

# Safety Exercises

These exercises require some dedication and self-discipline. Control of the balls is critical to your success in frustrating opponents. Once learned, these skills are yours to use, wherever you play.

## Cue Ball Speed Control

To be a better player and shooter, you have to master how hard and soft you hit the cue ball. This control is necessary for offensive as well as defensive shots. Offensively, knowing how control the speed you push the cue tip into the cue ball helps get shape for the next shot. Defensively, intentional cue ball speed control allows you to play shots with confidence and that the result matches your intention.

You only need to master these three soft speeds and three medium speeds. Once you own these shots, your results will be predictable and trustworthy.

### *Soft 1, Soft 2, Soft 3 Speeds*
Strive to get the cue ball within a few inches of the position shown.

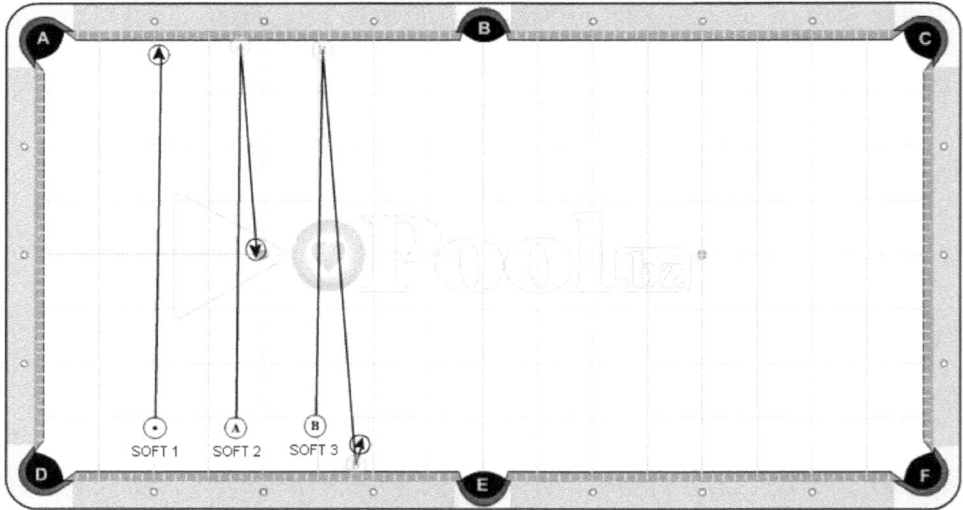

## Medium 1, Medium 2, Medium 3 Speeds

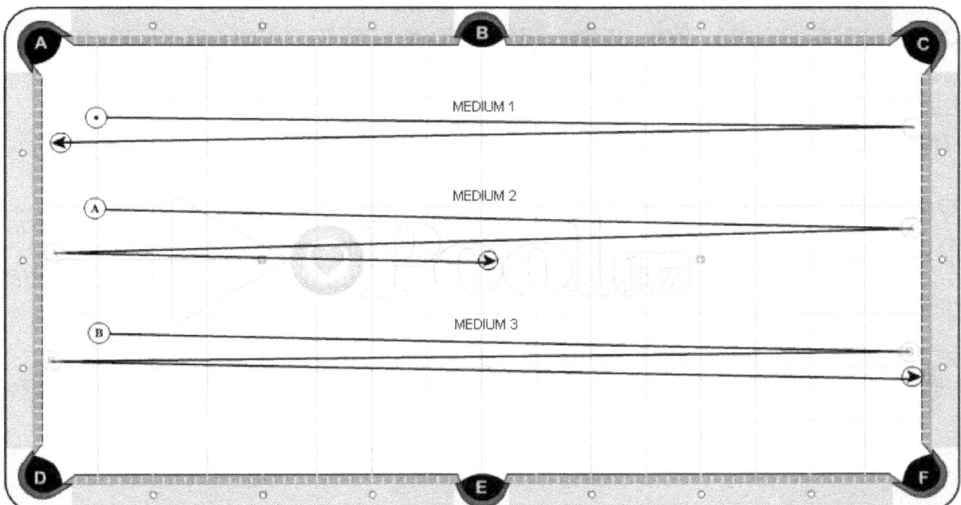

## Cue Ball Position Control

The next level of ball control is controlling where and how far the cue ball goes after it contacts an object ball. Being able to do this intentionally helps you consistently get the results you intended before the shot.

There are three ways that the cue ball runs out of energy, and you must get a feeling for how much energy will be lost in each situation.

- Amount of energy lost when the cue ball hits the object ball. The more full the hit, the more energy is transferred from the cue ball to the object ball. The more thin the hit, the more energy is kept with the cue ball.
- Amount of energy lost when the cue ball hits the cushions. The quality of the cushions can change from table to table. A few speed control shots will provide enough information to adjust for this.
- Amount of energy lost from rolling on the cloth. A few test rolls determine any differences between your regular table and the match table. Another technique is to rub your hand across the cloth. The less resistance, the further the balls will roll.

For these cue ball control exercises, use donuts (paper

reinforcement rings). This allows you to consistently position the balls so that shots can be repeated over and over until you get consistent results. Adjust the target location to different locations to get a "feel" for different distances and different contact (thin to full). Like the speed control shots, practice these until you can perform them at will.

### *One Cushion examples*
Try these shots into the object balls from thin to thick (i.e., 1/4 ball, 1/3 ball, and 1/2 ball). For thick contacts, use follow to help the cue ball roll in the direction and distance intended.

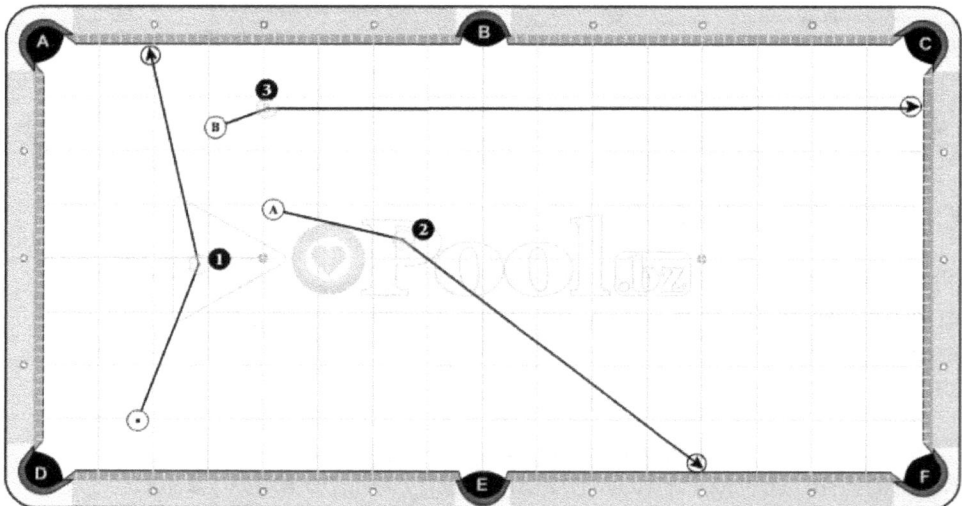

## *Two Cushion examples*
Do the same thin-to-thick object ball contacts.

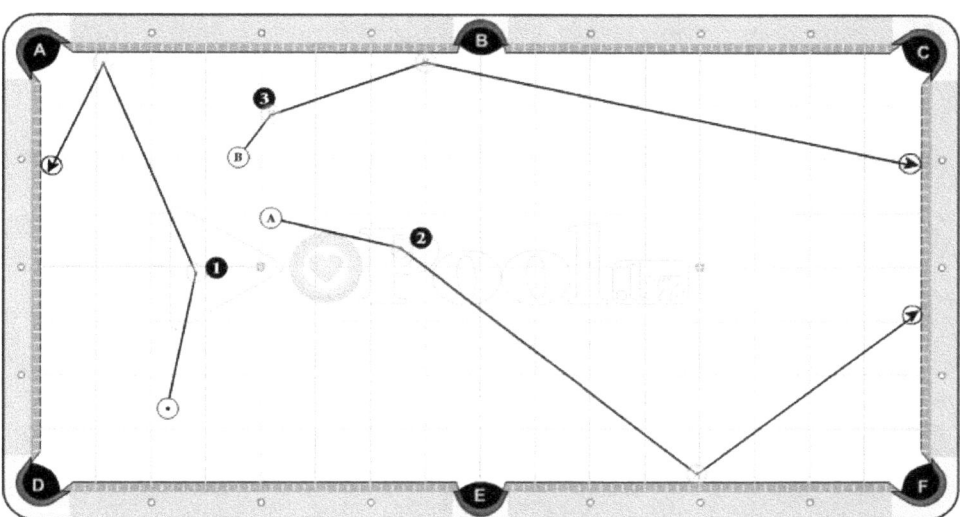

# Object Ball Position Control

There are playing situations where it is more important to control where the object ball stops rolling than where the cue ball ends up. You can always get a rough idea where the cue ball will go, but the necessary precision is necessary only for the object ball.

In an 8 Ball game, you can move one of your balls into a blocking position or use your ball kick your opponent's ball out of a good position. In 9 Ball, you can create an effective distance or bad angle safety.

The more skillful you become with object ball positioning, the more options available when analyzing table layouts. Over time, you will develop some complex game strategies and tactics that will be the despair of your opponents.

When you first start practicing this, put a sheet of paper on the table where you want the object ball to stop. As you get better, use a dollar bill.

## *One Cushion examples*
Start with using thin object ball contacts and get the cue ball to roll up against the cushion. Then move the cue ball position (right or left) in order to contact the object ball more full. You'll need to learn the angle off the object ball and the

effects of using follow at various speeds.

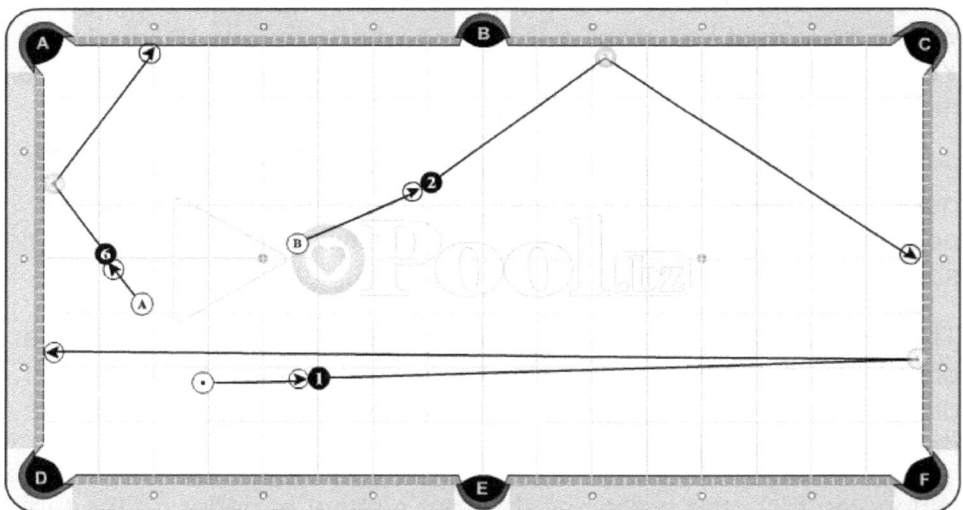

**Two Cushion examples**

Knowing how to carefully place the object ball in these examples can cause your opponent untold problems.

# Cue Ball Follow Control

There is the old saying, "Draw for show, follow for dough." This cool rhyme declares a valuable truth. It is always easier to control the cue ball with follow than with draw.

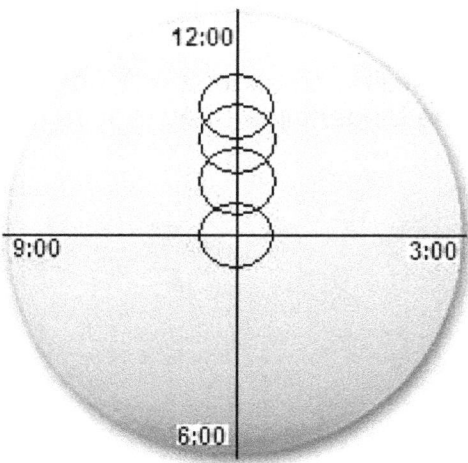

## Follow Control examples

On each target, use a piece of chalk to mark the target. Learn to slowly roll the cue ball into the target.

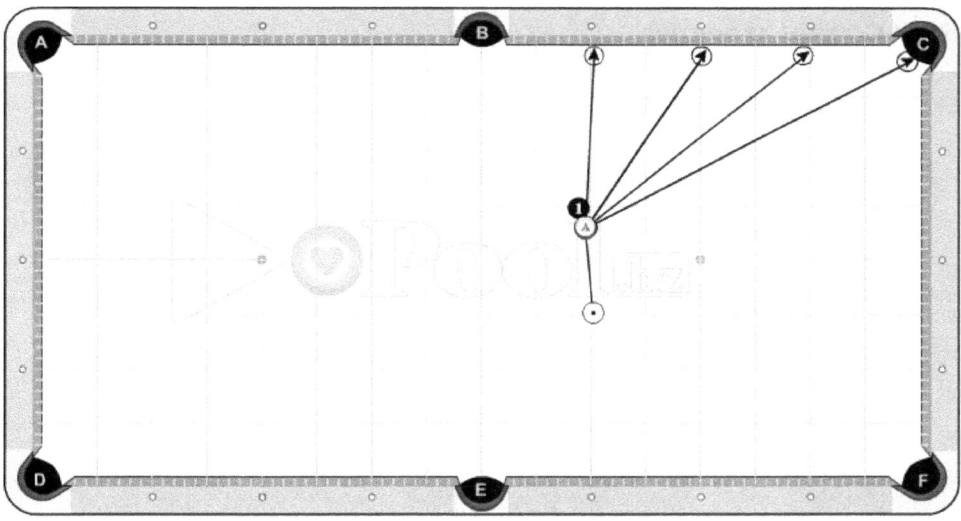

## Cue Ball Stun Control

For these exercises, use stun (ball is sliding on contact with object ball) to keep the cue ball rolling on the tangent line (may require some draw).

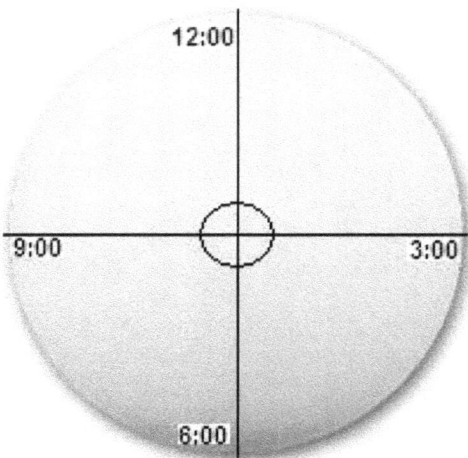

### *Stun Control examples*

For each target, use donuts, a small Post-it sheet or a chalk mark. Practice stopping the cue ball on each target.

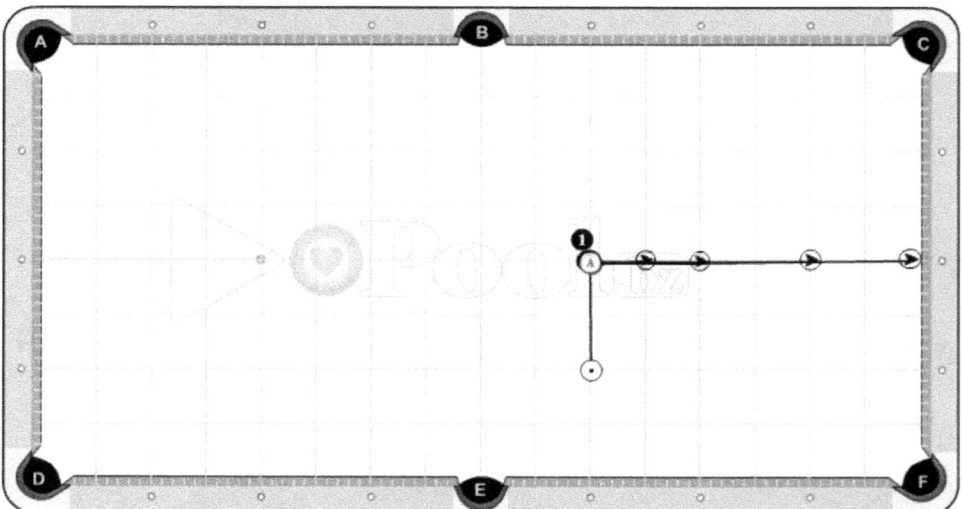

## Cue Ball Draw Control

Practice this until you have precise control. It will take a lot of work, but the improvement in your self-confidence will be significant. It is a major accomplishment to precisely control the cue ball. (P.S., the "secret" is to put the tip up close to the cue ball on the practice strokes, mark that cue tip contact point on the cue ball, and then use the correct Soft 1, 2, 3 speeds.)

### *Draw Control examples*

For each target, use donuts, a small Post-it sheet or a chalk mark. Practice stopping the cue ball on each target.

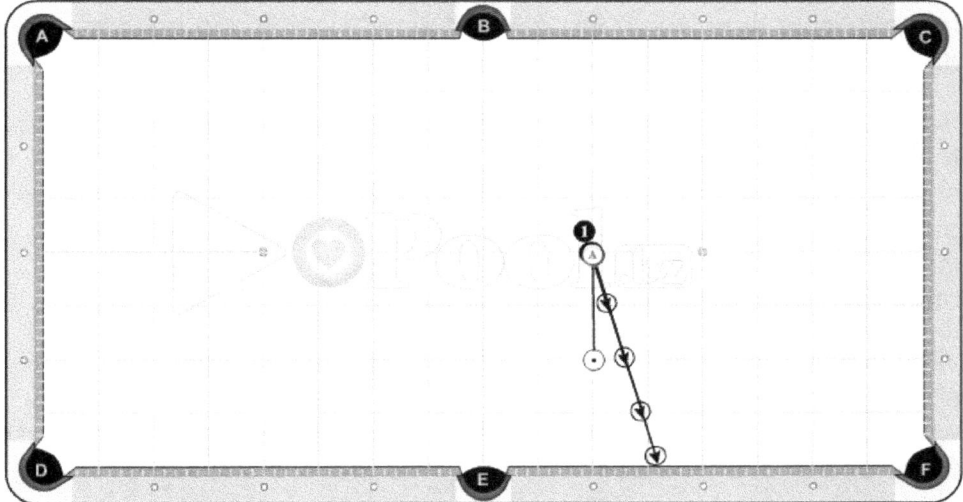

# Safety Basics

This section describes some defensive ideas to help you make good safety choices.

When you play a defensive shot, you are allowing your opponent to come to the table. This actually makes you choices easier. All you need to do is give him something he will not like. And if you wouldn't like it, that's the table you want to give him.

## Know Your Comfort/Chaos Zones

Let's define these two concepts: When you have a shot that is easy to make, that shot is in your "comfort zone". When you have a difficult shot - that shot is in your "chaos zone".

Before you choose a shot, look at the layout and decide what to do. If a shot is in your comfort zone, you can figure out what your next shot will be. If a shot is in your chaos zone, you can start figuring out how to play a safety. The basic rule of thumb for comfort zone is: you can make the ball at least 3 times out of 5 attempts. Every other shot falls within your chaos zone.

Why is this important? For you, it helps you decide when you should play a safety. When you choose a defensive shot, then you want to give your opponent a shot you don't like. Knowing this, you only need to push the balls into positions that are difficult for you to play.

You don't have to consider complicated and sophisticated defensive shots when you need a safety. Get your imagination under control and keep the options simple.

## Basic Defense & Safety Fundamentals

*Comfort-Chaos Zone example*

Set these shots up and test them for yourself. You really must have a thorough understanding of what you can (and cannot) do.

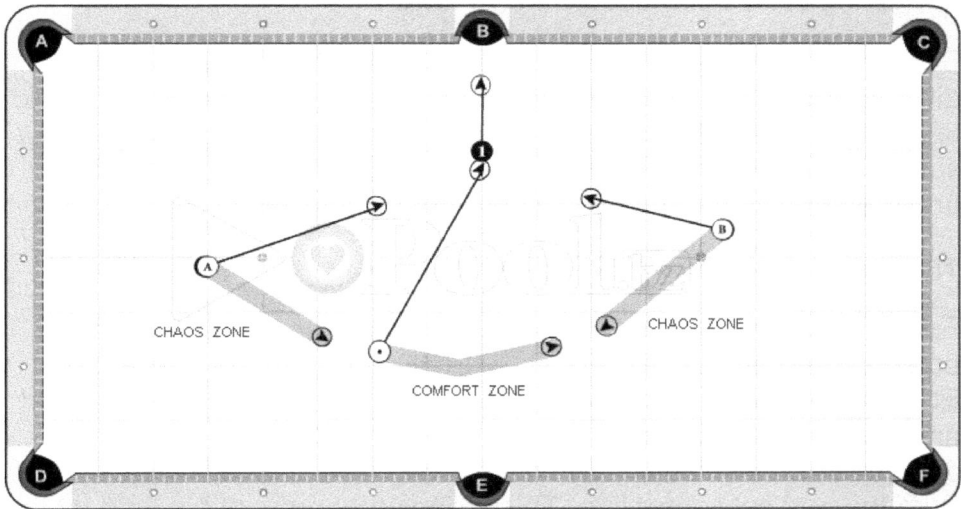

# Recognizing Opponent's Bad Habits

Sometimes you hear a top player say something like, "It doesn't matter who the opponent is – play the table." At that level of competition, it is a true statement. For the rest of us in the pool playing universe, playing the opponent will help win more games.

Every player has bad habits. For the better players, these are minor in nature and only affect certain types of shots. Regular players usually have several bad habits. Those bad habits keep them at their playing level, month after month and year after year.

Spotting common bad habits in your opponent improves your chances of winning. You know what situations that will lower his chances of success. This gives you more shooting opportunities. A number of common bad habits are identified below.

*The Slammer Banger*

This player likes to hit the cue ball much harder than necessary – much, much harder. The problem with this bad habit is that the ball can rattle the pocket and escape back onto the table. When a slower speed would have made the ball, this player simply can't stop himself.

## Basic Defense & Safety Fundamentals

Somewhere in his early playing lifetime, some equally ignorant player complimented him a few times. Because of this, this bad habit was accepted as "proper" playing. You can encourage this by appearing to be impressed with his "skill".

Some slammers appear to play sanely when the shots are not too difficult. But when the shot is tougher, he simply loses patience and uses high speed shots while secretly praying to the billiard gods for success (which rarely works). Give this player a lot of off-the-rail and distance shots and he will shoot himself to death.

### *The Happy Spinster*

For whatever reason, this player can't shoot the cue ball without putting some amount of "English" (that's "side" for you guys in England). Of course, this forces the cue ball to act strangely (squirt and swerve) which is very difficult to predict. The spinster usually does this unconsciously. The cue tip might be offside 1/4 to 1/2 tip from the vertical center line. This means that most of his long table shots will be missed.

Sometimes, this is done intentionally, in an attempt to imitate what the pros do to manage the cue ball. Of course, this player isn't willing to put the 6-10 hours of daily practice time for a few years to master English over any distance. When you play such an opponent, give him a lot of long shots. Most of these shots will be missed.

### *The Bad Fundamentalist*

This player with this handicap will never get good enough to become a serious competitor. Instead of a balanced stance with all body parts aligned in a stable platform, his feet, hands, head, and body positions will be misplaced. Every stroke will engage movement of multiple body parts – a definite no-no for trustworthy stroking.

Among the fundamental sins is feet alignment. This player can align the feet along the cue stick line. A small gust of wind would tip him over. Or, he'll grab the cue stick all the way back at the butt end and his stroke will freely avoid a straight movement. His elbow can stick out like a chicken wing or be so close to the body that the hand was to angle away for free movement.

This player will have great difficulty with object balls that are not close to the pocket. Leaving this shooter with a lot of long-distance shots is almost the same as teasing a younger sister or brother. Fortunately, there aren't any adults around to make you stop, so you might as well enjoy yourself.

### *The Whiner*

This player is easy to spot. He continually complains about something or other. Leave him an easy shot to pocket and he'll screw up position on the next shot, and loudly complain. Of course, the fact that he didn't consider how to properly play the shot has nothing to do with his new problem.

For this type of player, you need several "supportive" responses. Constantly and continuously agree with him. Alternate this with sympathetic words on every poor result. When you leave him bad, apologize. All of these help keep is focus on his problems. He'll be so busy looking for reasons to complain that he won't have any energy left to develop positive plans. You have to wonder, if this guy complains so much, why is he playing pool?

For this player, temporarily stop playing offensively to concentrate on leaving several tough shots in a row. Apologize each time to get him started moaning and groaning. After that, he pretty much self-destructs. If he does win the occasional game, it's because you allowed him to win.

### *The Distance Dilettante*

This player is pathologically afraid of long shots. His self-confidence drops off the further away it is to the target pocket.

On missing any long green shot, he casually mentions how much he hates shooting long shots. Even if the object ball is in the pocket, from far away, it is 50/50 shot. Even if made, the layout usually leaves him tough.

Once your opponent reveals this as a weakness, be very generous in leaving long green shots. You can tell how poorly he will play the shot by how loudly he declares is worries about the shot's success. Feel free to torture him, even at the expense of passing up easy shots.

## Basic Defense & Safety Fundamentals

### The Raker Faker

These players are far more common than you might believe. For you (being the intelligent player that you are), using the mechanical bridge is not be a big problem. After all, the bridge can be positioned as close to the cue ball as you want and can easily align the cue with the correct angle. What's not to like?

Yet, many players consider the rake to be proof of weakness and (if a guy), being a girly man. They will stretch and twist and even hurt themselves – just to avoid using it. When you know your opponent suffers this malady, give him many of these shots. After 3 or 4 of these problem shots, he will begin indicating some level of irritation or upsetness. (It's always an easy win when your opponent gets pissed off at himself during the game.)

### The Cushion Impaired

Any player who suffers this problem are fun to watch. When the cue ball is close to the cushion, he always jacks up the cue stick like he is trying to stab the cue ball into the table. Because this is a difficult and painful position to hold, the shot is quickly stroked, usually within two or three seconds. This, of course, messes up the shot even more.

Give this player a lot of cushion shots, even if you have to pass up an easy shot. Shooting continuous jacked-up shots makes an opponent tired. If not too bright, he won't even realize you are purposely giving him these difficulties.

### The Anxious Rusher

This player has absolutely no patience. He reveals himself by constantly fidgeting and twitching when forced to wait more than 10 seconds. Another indicator is the quickness which he moves from the sidelines to the table after you miss a shot. The balls will still be rolling and he is aligning himself for his shot. If seated, he is on the edge of the chair. If standing, he shifts his weight from foot to foot.

This type of player gives you several advantages. He will always take the easiest shot available. He won't consider how to play a shot for position. If given a tough position, he does not consider playing a defensive shot. You can count on him always paying offense regardless of the table layout.

You can easily increase his anxiety by constantly taking your time on deciding the shot and more time shooting the shot. Over several games, he can get so agitated about getting a shot that his brain will simply stop working.

### *The Bad Banker*

It takes a lot of practice to consistently make bank shots. For most players, even the simplest cross side or cross corner bank cannot be pocketed more than 2 or 3 times out of 10 tries. On top of that problem is the difficulty to control the cue ball for the next shot even if the bank is successful.

With these odds, constantly leaving bank shots for your opponent gives you many opportunities to win. The very untrustworthiness of the shot will cause your opponent a certain amount of frustration. Do a mix of cross side banks with long table banks – just to frustrate him.

## Dead Zones

There are areas of the table, known as dead zones. When an object ball is within these zones, pocketing the ball is much more difficult. The shaded areas in the following table layout define these dead zones. When a target object ball is within these areas, there are very small areas in which you must place the cue ball in order to properly shoot the ball.

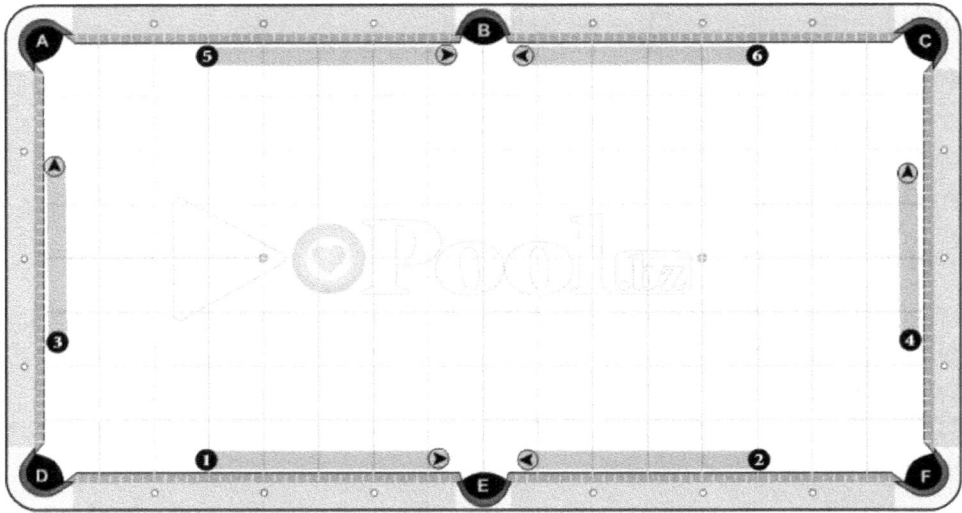

In 8 Ball, when your opponent avoids improving his table by leaving dead zone balls for later, he reveals a playing style weakness you can take advantage. Essentially, any of his balls in a dead zone becomes insurance. That means he cannot run out the table. Eventually, when he is forced to play a dead zone ball, you will come to the table with a chance to win.

If your ball is in a dead zone, get it out in the open or near a pocket early in the game – while playing a defensive shot. Here are some 8 Ball examples on how to properly play balls in a dead zone. Do these shots early in the game, so that these balls are easily made for your final run-out.

*How to Handle Your Own 8 Ball Dead Zone examples*

## Dangers of "Ball-in-Hand"

However, you got the ball-in-hand opportunity, that seeming gift can turn out to be poisoned. The surprise and pleasure seems to affect many players' abilities to think clearly. Watch several games between other players. Observe how each reacts when presented with a ball-in-hand. If obviously pleased, you will observe that they usually will not and cannot make more than two balls.

It's good when your opponent suffers this problem. In 8 Ball, you can actually use this to your advantage in the early game. Use an illegal shot to break open a difficult cluster, or move several of your balls into better positions. To do this, either intentionally scratch the cue ball, or accidently hit his ball first. With so many balls left on the table, he won't be able to run out. The one or two balls he makes will help clear up the table – which makes it easier for you to get to the win.

When you get a ball-in-hand, treat the situation with worried nervousness. Your goal is to make at least three balls. To do this, take a long time to calculate the pattern. Consider multiple options from various angles and cue ball speeds. As much as possible, use slow natural roll and stun shots.

When you make your decision, carefully position the cue ball. Take your time to choose the right speed and aim. Only then make the stroke. This will get you into position for the next shot. Apply the same level of seriousness. With this attitude, you can expect to make at least 3 and more balls when your opponent gives you ball-in-hand.

## Stupid Hero (& Superhero) Shots

Want to be a hero? In pool, it's easy to try, but hard to succeed. Pick any low percentage shot. Declare your intention to successfully pocket the ball and shoot. If you make it (however rarely), you get to walk around the table accepting the applause of supporters and enjoy the groans of your enemies. But if you miss, you must suffer the jeers of your buddies and cheers of your opposition.

Why put yourself in a situation where the chances of failure are astronomical? Why attempt a shot that makes people question your intelligence? Actually, when faced with a shot that requires a math computer to calculate the odds of success, the smart decision is to play defensively. Applying this process to any bad layout will help you win more games.

Feel free to continuously encourage your opponent to attempt those silly hero shots and he will help you win. Let him play the fool, while you play carefully. Make sure to wish your opponent better luck next time. (This encourages his behavior.)

Avoid such players as a partner. There is no sense in getting frustrated over his ignorance, and you don't need to educate him on smarter playing decisions.

## Ensuring Insurance Balls

It might seem strange to consider insurance to be part of the Green Game; it does describe a useful condition that can help win games. Anything in a table layout that slows down or stops an opponent from running out the table benefits you.

Insurance is any layout that prevents a player from running out the table to the win. It can be any of these layouts:

- one or more balls in a dead zone
- balls in a cluster

- balls at opposite ends of the table
- an angle on an easy shot that prevents getting shape on the next ball

**8 Ball Insurance**

Most players tend to focus on making the easy balls first and leave the difficult problem shots for last. If there isn't an existing situation early in the game, you can take a turn at the table and create one or more insurance situations with your opponent's balls. Do this with a carom off your ball into his to push the ball into a bad situation (for him).

You want insurance against your opponent. If your balls are tied up in insurance situations, use the early game to open them up (while playing defensively).

*8 Ball Insurance examples*

This layout shows 8 insurance problems for the cue ball position (both solids and stripes).

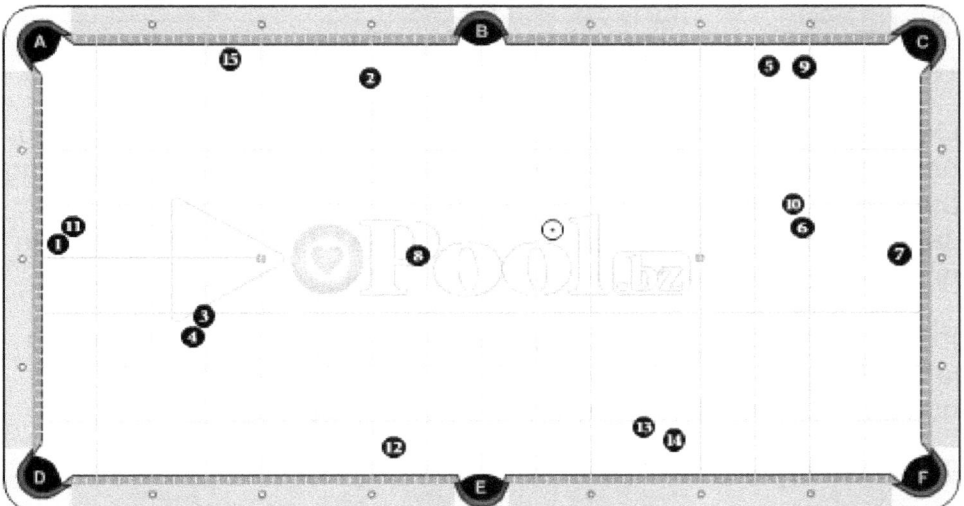

**9 Ball Insurance**

When playing a better player, insurance balls ensure that you will come back to the table. The following are examples of insurance situations:

- A higher ball blocks a lower ball.

## Basic Defense & Safety Fundamentals

- Sequential balls at opposite ends of the table
- High balls (7, 8, 9) tied up in a cluster.

*9 Ball Insurance examples*

This layout presents multiple insurance situations for the cue ball position.

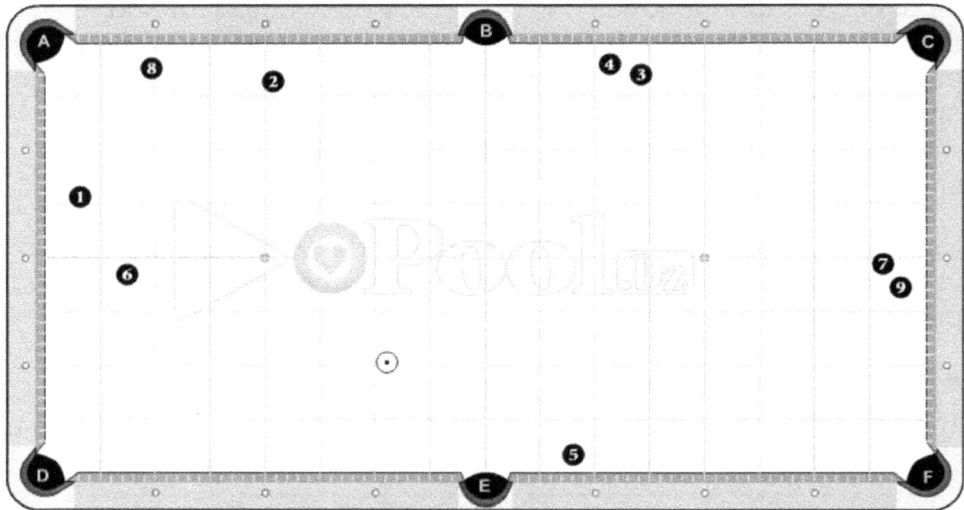

## How to Win Safety Battles

Occasionally, you will compete against a smarter shooter. Like you, he is aware of the need to play defensively when necessary. During the competition, the two of you will become engaged in multiple safety battles. As each player comes to the table, the intention is to prevent the opponent from having a chance to advance the game.

In these battles, it is the player who makes a position mistake who loses the game. If you have practiced the safety exercises in this book, the person who loses should be your opponent.

**8 Ball Safety Battle Tips**

Use these general guidelines:

- If you are on the 8 ball and your opponent has several balls to go, simply move the 8 ball close to a pocket to win on your next turn.
- If your opponent is on the 8 ball, regardless of the layout, play to prevent him from having a shot.

- If both on the 8 ball and you don't have a good shot to win, push the 8 ball around to set up distance and bad angle safeties.
- Be patient.

**9 Ball Safety Battle Tips**

Apply these considerations:

- Play all bank shots as a two-way.
- Shoot any 40-70% shot as a two-way.
- In the end-game, precision placement becomes more important.
- Among the variety of safety options, choose the easiest.
- Be patient.

## How to Make Safety Mistakes

The purpose of playing a safety is to prevent your opponent from having a shot and winning the game – a simple enough goal. Your shot doesn't have to be perfect, just tough or difficult. But, you can make mistakes.

Unless you have spent a lot of practice time precisely placing the cue ball or object ball, the occasional mistake will occur. Some of them you might recover from, but there is no reason to make your opponent's life a little easier.

There are two types of mistakes – mental (the shot selection) and physical (the shot execution).

Here are some mental errors:

- Not thinking – grabbing the first possibility you see.
- Thinking small – only considering a few possibilities.
- Not figuring out the amount of energy to put into the cue ball.
- Hoping and fantasizing results rather than working out the details.
- Not calculating ball paths and distances before the shot.
- Laziness – assuming a truth without any basis in reality.
- Selecting shots beyond your competence.

Here are some execution errors:

- Too much energy.
- Too little energy.
- Incorrect angle off the object ball.
- Incorrect angle off the rail.
- Incorrect cue ball spin.
- Not mentally practicing the shot.
- Unplanned object ball contact.
- Miscue.

The truth is – you will make mistakes. It's part of your learning process. Always calculate opportunities from simple to complex. Start with the simplest possible approach with the least possible cue ball movement. This will reduce the possible errors. The best all-around rule for the majority of your shots is, "Shoot soft and softer."

## How to Learn from Playing Errors

If you don't want to improve your game, the best way to do this is to pretend that mistakes never happened. You can also blame mistakes on the billiard gods, the table, the cue, or anything else – except yourself.

Mental and physical mistakes are very common. This is reality of playing any sport. The more difficult the shot, the greater are the chances of failure.

A bar-banger does not accept responsibility for mistakes (probably due to genetics). Apparently, there aren't enough brain cells available for thinking.

If you want to become the "Intelligent Shooter", the making of a mistake is an opportunity to figure out what should have been done, not an excuse for complaining to the world. it doesn't matter whether there were contributing factors (equipment, others, etc.).

A slight change in attitude can help you become a better player much more quickly. The attitude modification must be done all of the time – regardless of how good you get.

When analyzing poor results, there are several areas to be considered:

- Shot analysis – not selecting the best shot for the table layout.
- Pre-shot setup – not lining up, not calculating the correct speed for the stroke, not aiming correctly.
- Shot execution – not shooting at the right speed, not following through.

As you correct one error (analysis, setup, execution), another error reveals itself. For example, you learn cue ball speed control, to then discover that your stoke needs straightening. When that is fixed, you might realize that your head alignment was helping you miss.

Always fix one problem at a time. This requires patience. Sometimes it can take months to fix one problem. But, once resolved, it is fixed for life.

## How to Select the Best Shot

Whether playing a defensive or offensive shot, it is very important to select the best shot for the table layout. The actual selection will depend on how the balls are laid out on the table and your experience in table analysis.

At first glance, this analysis might seem to require that you consider hundreds and even thousands of possible shots. Like many situations that appear to be complicated at first look, you can make the choices much easier by following some simple guidelines.

- Determine the purpose of the shot.
  - If offensive, what speeds and spins can pocket the target object ball and get shape on the next? Can you do it?
  - If defensive, what table layout will make life difficult for your opponent?
- Consider simple options first. If your brain starts hurting, it's too complicated. Back off and look for easy solutions.
- Select two or three possible shots. Then consider the possible paths of the cue ball and object balls. Choose the one that is the easiest to shoot.
- Remember where you want the balls to stop. That tells you the

speed for the shot.
- If successful, mentally replay the shot selection and execution process, and congratulate yourself.
- If a failure, stop and replay the selection and imagine how you should have made the shot.

It does take some practice and intentional effort to work on these. Basically, you are creating a fantasy shot. Always compare the reality to the fantasy. If too far apart, choose simpler shots. Using these experiences to become a better player takes time and close attention to your experiences. As you get better, your shot choices more closely match up fantasy to reality.

# Basic Defense & Safety Fundamentals

## Hidden Ball Shadows

A shadow zone is the table area behind one or more blocking balls. It is the key element of a hidden ball safety type. Any target ball within the shadow zone can be reached either by jumping the blocking ball (if rules allow) or shooting the cue ball off one or more cushions.

When a hidden ball safety is successful, there are one or more blocking balls between the cue ball and target object ball. This requires the opponent to consider less comfortable shooting choices, such as kicking from one or more rails in order to make a legal hit.

When setting up your hidden ball safety shot, determine how big the shadow is. Some table areas in a hidden zone are so small that it is nearly impossible to get the ball into position. The easiest process is to select target areas that require the smallest amount of travel.

### *Cue Ball Shadow examples*

The closer the cue ball is to the blocking ball, the bigger the shadow. Look at the shadows on the 11 ball, 6 ball, and 3 ball.

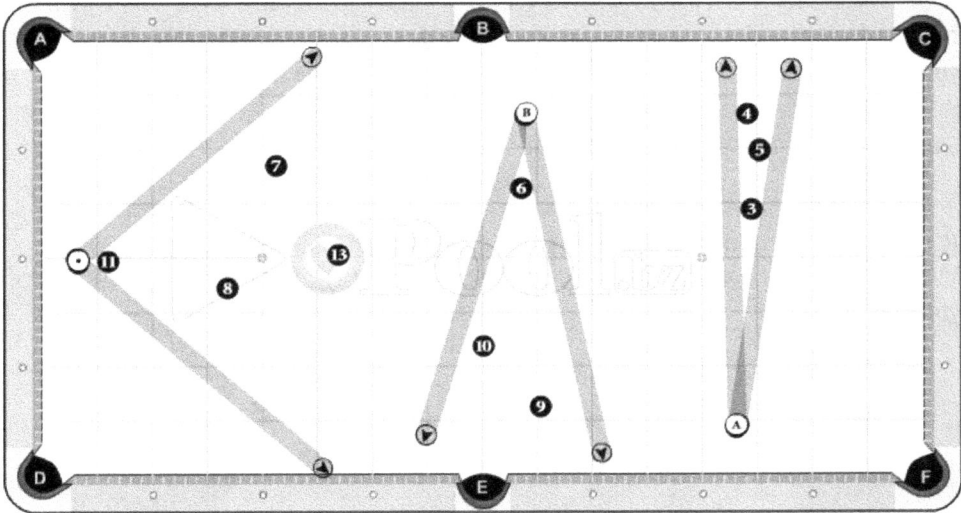

### *Object Ball Shadow examples*

You can shoot object balls to stop behind other object balls. Below are successful results. Object balls hide the 13 ball, 15 ball, and 11 ball.

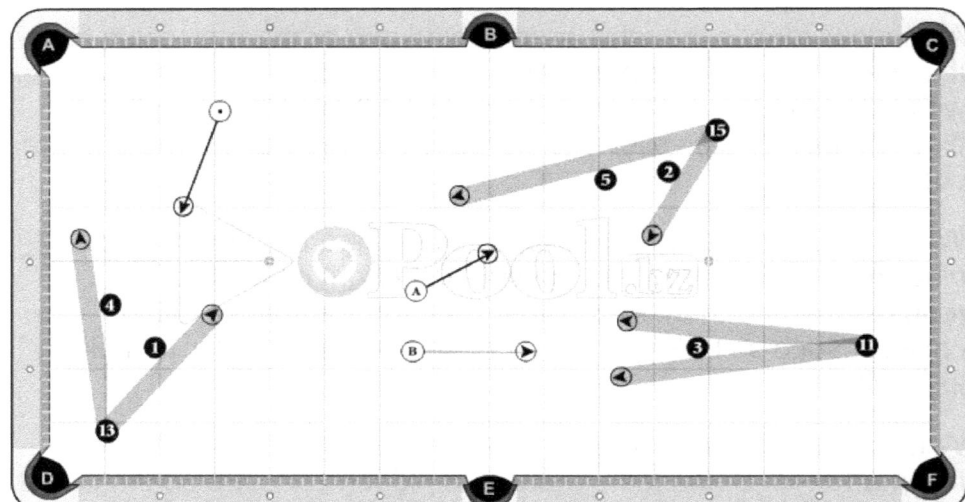

When you place the cue ball closer to a blocking object ball, the size of the shadow zone is increased. If the easier angles to kick at the target object ball are blocked, the hidden ball safety is even more difficult.

Several blocking balls can be combined to create shadows that hide much larger areas of the table. Putting the cue ball or object ball in the shadow of several balls requires less precision. When planning a hidden ball safety, look first for table areas where several balls can together create a large shadow zone, then figure out how to get the ball into that area.

The "wall of balls" requires much less precision. It's a larger area for the ball to roll into and doesn't require great ball control skills. When there are a lot of balls on the table, look first for a grouping of balls.

## Wall of Balls Shadow Zone example

This shows how multiple balls can be combined to create a much larger shadow zone.

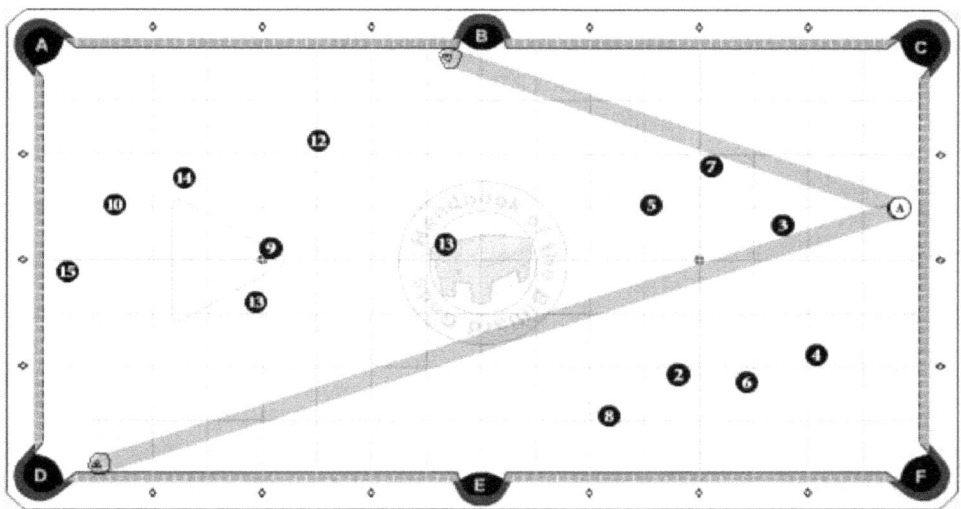

# Safety Tactics

When going on the offense, it helps to know how to pocket balls and get shape on the next ball, and so. But more important, you have to look at the table layout and figure out what can be done within your skill. Your analysis and response to the table layout are the tactical decisions. This section describes what can be done.

## Tactical Options & Choices

Just as offensive efforts require tactics, so do defensive efforts. When you decide to play a safety, your result you want is quite easy – make sure your opponent doesn't have an easy shot. With that simple purpose, your choices are extensive.

The 8 Ball and 9 Ball examples below demonstrate the basic concept. Study these examples to understand just how flexible your options are.

### *8 Ball Tactical Safety Options*
Off the 2 ball - a soft roll & half ball hit works. Off the 3 ball – a soft left spin works. Off the 6 ball – a glancing 1/4 or 1/3 ball hit works.

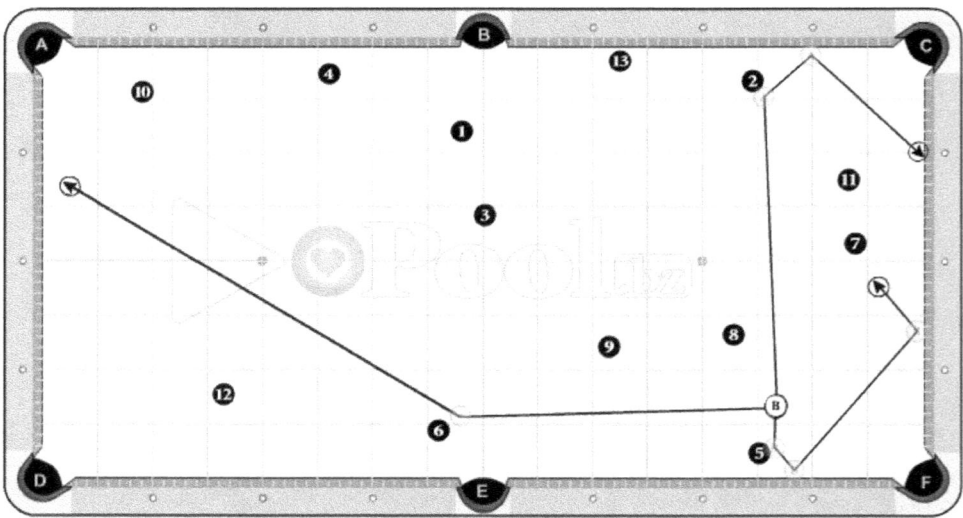

### *9 Ball Tactical Safety examples*
For these 9 Ball safeties, there are 3 options to play off the 4 ball – a stun shot, 1/2 ball hit, and 1/4 ball hit on the 4 ball.

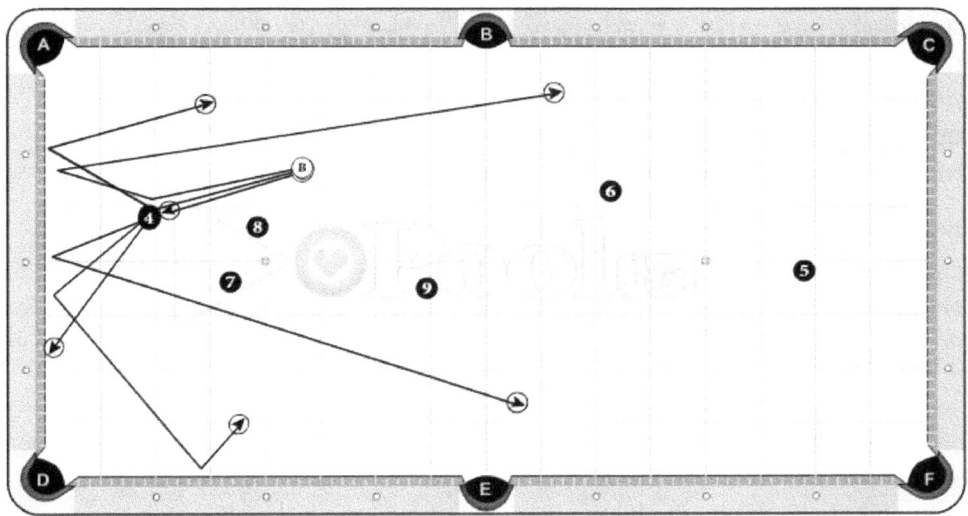

## Smart Missing

There are table layout situations where you do not want to make a ball. Just because the shot in front of you is easy, doesn't mean that the next shot (or the shot after) can be pocketed to advance towards the win. The problem ball or balls can be a cluster, bad location, blocked balls, etc.). You might want to let your opponent take care of the problem.

This means you have to intentionally miss the shot. If the shot is easy, you can complain that something got in your eye. This is a good tactic, especially if he is not a smart player (like you).

Here are a couple of common situations that can allow you to use the smart miss:

- No way to get position for the next ball.
- No shot on the next ball.
- If you break up the last cluster, your opponent wins.
- A cluster is so nasty you want your opponent to take it.

### 8 Ball Smart Miss

In 8 Ball, it's a good idea to use a soft shot to ensure that your object ball stays close by the pocket. This becomes a backup shot when your opponent is forced to give the table back. This backup ball can be used to get shape on other balls.

## Basic Defense & Safety Fundamentals

A smart miss can be made any time in the game. Here is a common tactic. Use the first four turns at the table to setup a ball near a corner pocket while leaving a poor position for your opponent. By the time your opponent realizes what you are doing, he is almost certain to lose the game.

### *8 Ball smart miss example*

On this layout, your opponent can easily make the 11 ball, but cannot get good shape on the 13 ball. Each of these three "smart misses" set up the object ball for an easy shot the next time you come to the table. You don't want to break out the 3 ball. That is something for your opponent to do.

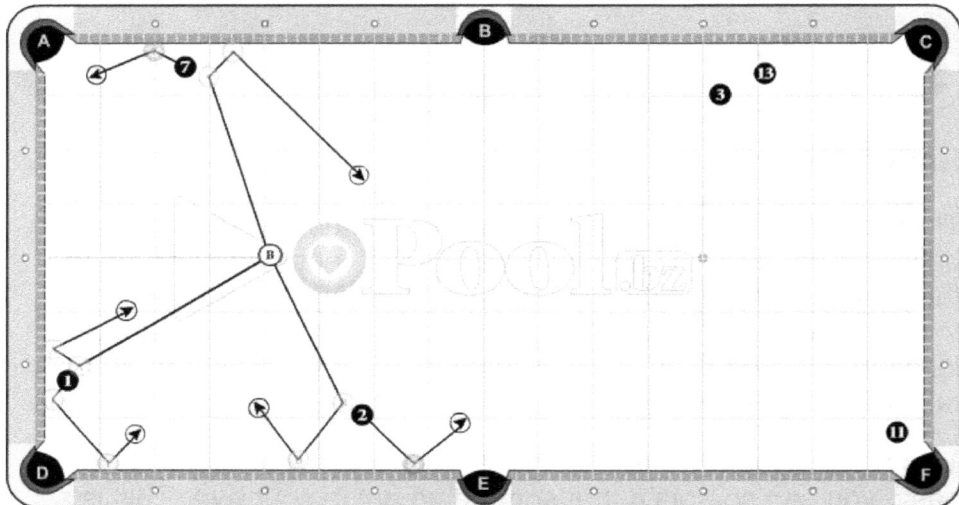

### 9 Ball Smart Miss

In 9 Ball, your opponent must shoot the lowest number ball on the table. When higher numbered balls are tied up in a cluster or in bad locations, it is a good idea to let your opponent shoot at those balls. Give him an easy shot with one ball to pocket, which then forces him to address the problem balls.

It is a tactical mistake to open up problem balls yourself. Instead, allow your opponent an opportunity to make that tactical error. And the more opportunities you give your opponent to help you, the greater your chances to win. When you have an opponent who can't resist an easy shot, you can control him at will.

## 9 Ball smart miss example

In these examples, you are "giving" your opponent an easy shot on the 6, but with an impossible shot on the 7 ball. This type of "smart miss" forces your opponent to handle the problem you don't want to shoot.

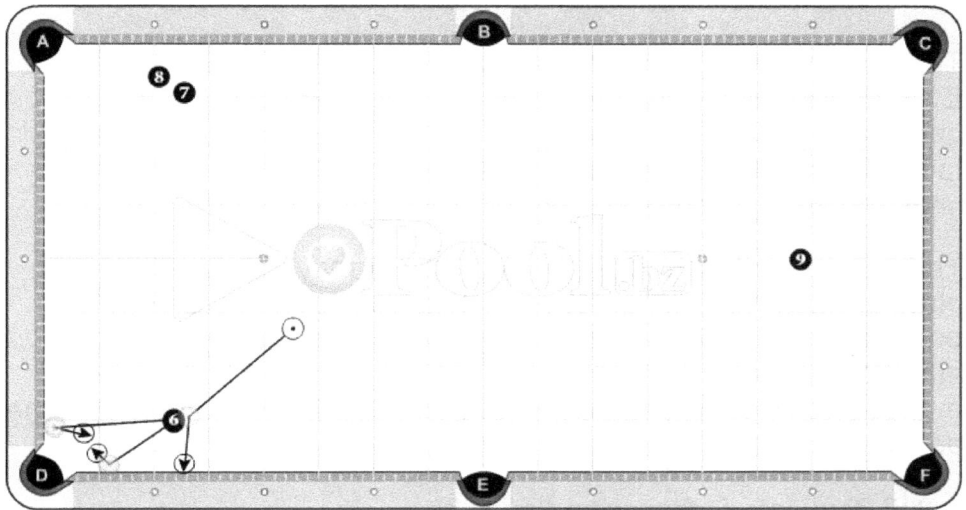

## Bank into a Safety

Generally, banks are considered to be low percentage shots. Not only is it difficult to consistently pocket the object ball, it is not that easy to control the cue ball and where it goes and stops.

This makes the problems of banking an object ball twice as difficult. Even if you pocket the object ball, can you also calculate the necessary cue ball speed to get shape for the next shot? When facing a difficult shot, most players tend to concentrate only the shot and not on where the cue ball will go after contact.

The sum total of these calculations may or may not be within your playing capabilities. When faced with a bank shot, consider the possibilities of intentionally missing. You can concentrate your attention on positioning either the cue ball or object ball. This makes the shooting decision an easier calculation. There is also the advantage that you are really playing a defensive shot.

### *8 Ball Bank into Safety examples*
1 ball – (cross corner) stun on the cue ball. 2 ball – (long table) follow. 6 ball – (long table, cross corner) stun.

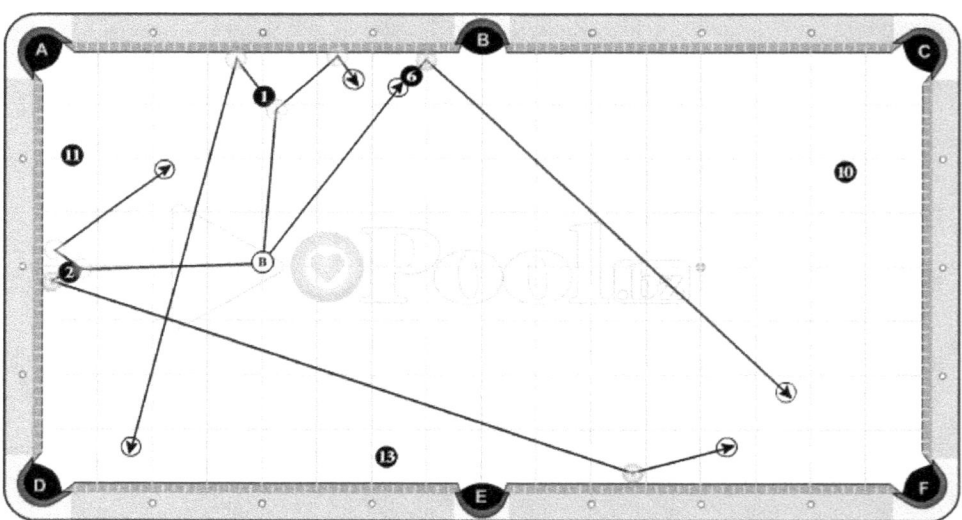

## 9 Ball Bank into Safety examples

These three examples put the object ball into a tough location for your opponent (cross side, long table, and long table cross side).

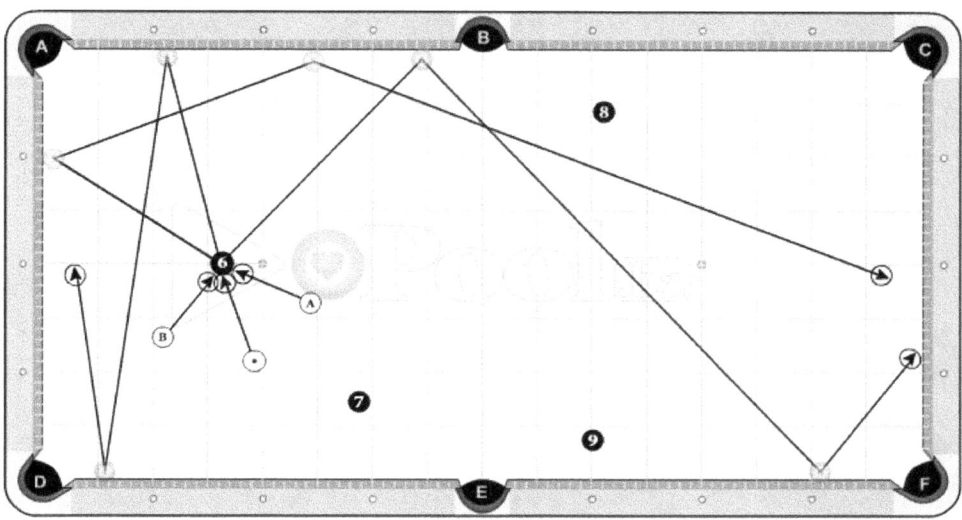

# Creating Pocket Blockers

This is an excellent 8 Ball tactical tool. It isn't necessary to make the object ball. Leave it near a pocket to be made later. The result also blocks the pocket for your opponent. You can set these balls up early in the game. Usually, your opponent won't realize what is going on until after you have blocked three pockets.

Most players tend to leave tough shots for later – after all the easy shots are made. When your opponent follows this strategy, he has informed you that he is easier to beat.

You follow different playing tactics. Basically, don't allow your opponent to control your game. During the early game, if your opponent has a ball blocking any pocket, either combo the ball into the pocket (if in the jaws) or use your object ball to kick his ball away. Of course, you make sure that your ball is now the blocker.

## 8 Ball – 3 examples

Each of these examples will irritate your opponent

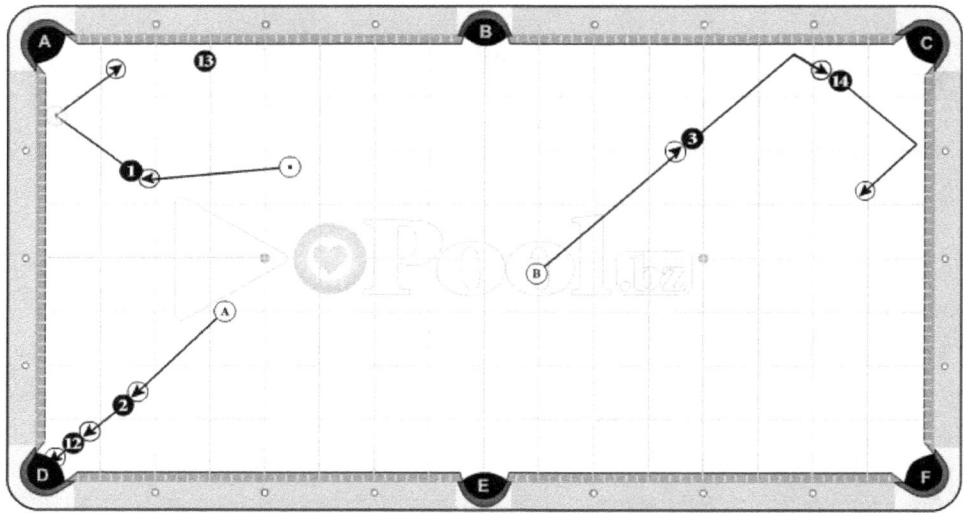

# Figuring BPI (balls per inning) Average

As much as each of us wishes we had perfect shooting skills, the truth is – we all have a built-in limitation. Like baseball players at bat, hitting averages are an excellent predictor of performance. A batter with a .254 who comes up to bat 4 times in a game, will average one hit. Yes, there will be times when he can do two or even three. But the average says one hit per four times at bat. Averages don't lie.

Pool players (no matter how good or bad) also have that limitation. In baseball, it is the batting average. In pool, it is BPI (balls per inning). That is the average number of balls made over any period of time. Some innings can be higher, some will be lower.

Here is how to get a working number. Over two or three games, count the total number of balls you pocketed and divide that by the number of innings. That BPI is your average. The number can go up or down a bit over time, but it's pretty much what you're stuck with.

How can you use BPI to your benefit? Well for one thing, if your BPI is 2.5 and there are 7 balls on the table to be pocketed, the chances of running out are very small. But, if there are 3 balls left on the table (in reasonable locations), you should be able to run out. With 7 balls on the table, eventually you will get out of position and forced to play a safety. Knowing this, you can keep your expectations firmly based on reality. It also frees you to decide when you want to leave your opponent a rough table layout.

How can you use your opponent's BPI against him? This also uses the same calculations. If he has 6 balls to a run-out and his BPI is 2.2, let him have a couple of easy shots. You know for a certainty that he will have to turn the table back to you.

Knowing your BPI and your opponent's BPI puts you in control of the game. You can decide when and how you let him shoot. That provides some predictability on when you will come back to the table.

At first, you might be a little nervous about using BPI averages in a match. It doesn't take long to realize how useful BPI can be in making playing decisions.

A note of *warning*: don't make this knowledge available to your opponent. A player short on sportsmanship might take his limitations personally and blame you. Continuously teasing an opponent about his BPI makes him less willing to compete with you in the future.

It is better for you to underestimate your real BPI. To confirm your "real" BPI, perform this exercise:

1. If you think your BPI is 3.0, toss four balls on the table.
2. Start with ball in hand.
3. Record balls pocketed in a single inning.
4. Do this 10 times.

If your BPI is truly 3.0, in five of the 10 times, you should make all four balls. If you didn't, your BPI is a smaller number. Regardless of the real number, it's better to know the truth than continue lying to yourself. Many players believe themselves to be a better player than they really are. If you keep your expectations close to reality, you can make better tactical decisions. By all means, encourage your opponents to believe in their unrealistic skills.

## End-game Tactics

In 8 Ball, the end-game begins when one or both players are down to 2 or 3 balls or there are only five or six balls on the table. In 9 Ball, the end-game starts at the 6 or 7 ball.

During the end-game, the winner is usually determined by who makes the last positioning mistake – either the cue ball rolls badly, or the object ball doesn't obey the shooter's intentions. If you know this going into the end-game, you can double your chances of winning. Basically, you concentrate on avoiding mistakes and encourage your opponent to make mistakes.

Basically, if you can't run out to the win, make absolutely sure your opponent cannot win with the table layout you leave. Let him make a mistake that you can use to win.

As a reminder, here are tactics that help your opponent make a mistake:

- Freeze the cue ball against a rail.
- Use the dead zones.
- Offer bank shots.
- Far, far away is good.
- Bad angles are always a plus.
- When going on the offense, play the last couple of balls as a two-way.

Above all - be patient. Until your opponent hands you the opportunity to win, take your time designing each defensive shot. Continue playing "keep away". Give your opponent every opportunity to make mistakes and give you a generous gift.

## Use Hangers as Traps

Hangers are object balls that sit in or very close to the jaws of any pocket (usually corner pockets and sometimes side pockets). Unless it is the game winning ball, giving your opponent a hanger can help you win the game.

First, he will be distracted by the hanger. During every shot, even if he doesn't play it, it will tempt his attention. (This is a nice way for him to waste his brain power.)

Second, hangers are dangerous. Pocketing the ball is so easy, that your opponent will forget to carefully plan his shape. It really is pretty tough to get shape from a hanger.

If you don't believe this, watch a few games between your buddies. When a hanger comes up, count how many times the player can get the cue ball into position for the next shot.

Once you realize what a trap the hanger is, you can allow your opponent to have these shots. To demonstrate just how careful you must be to handle these shots, use this exercise to improve your ability to get shape.

### *Hanger Exercise*

Use this exercise to improve your positioning skills so that a hanger will not be a trap for you. Exercise 1: pocket the 1 ball, get shape on and pocket the 2 ball. Exercise 2: Set up the cue ball and 1 ball, and then get shape on the 3 ball. Continue for the other object ball locations. In three tries on each ball position, count how many times you are successful.

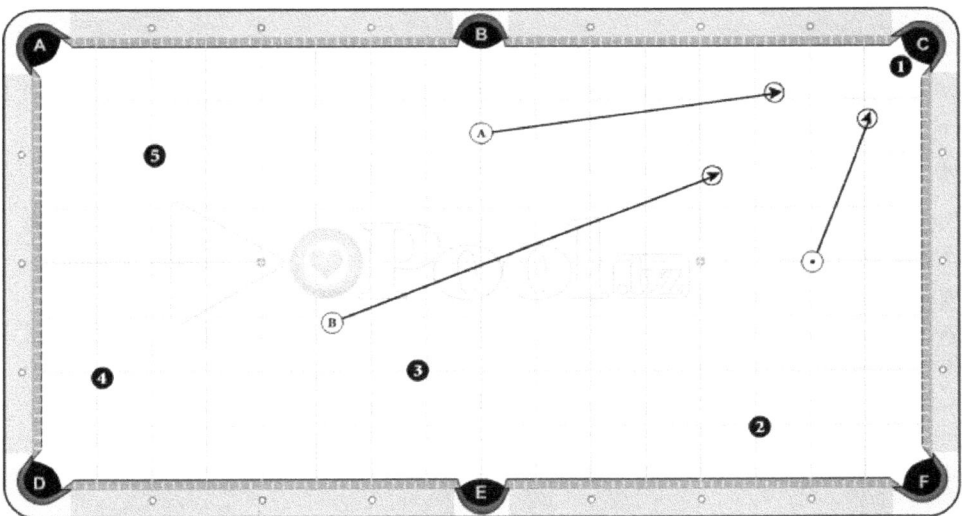

## How to Shoot Two-Way Shots

You are going to face many tough shots during competitions. Some of those shots will be low-percentage. But the rewards (improved chances to win) can make the shot worth trying. However, because the shot is low-percentage, you have to take further precautions.

This is the reason to go through the extra effort required for the "two-way" shot.

The "two-way" shot offers a best of both worlds opportunity. If the target object ball is pocketed, you have another shooting opportunity. If the object ball is missed, your opponent has a less than friendly table layout. Not every problem shot offers the opportunity to play a "two-way". But when the layout allows the possibility, you can take advantage. The more experiences in using "two-way" shots, the better you get at recognizing an opportunity.

Cue ball speed control is very important. You want to know where the cue ball and the object ball will stop in either circumstance. You basically have to figure out three possible shots. The first is if the ball is pocketed, the second possibility is if you miss the object ball to the left side of the pocket, and the third for missing the object ball to the right.

This calculation process can be difficult at first. Practicing is necessary. Knowing how to play such shots helps you get better at predicting results.

The trick with two-way shots is to make three calculations for the cue ball. The first, what happens if successful; second, failure to the right side of the pocket; and third, failure on the left side of the pocket?

Not every situation can be handled this way. About half of the time, it won't matter whether you make or miss the ball. Your opponent will have some kind of shot. However, for those other shots, it is worth calculating possible realities. If it gets too difficult to work out, just go for a "smart miss".

## "Two-way" example

You can see that the cue ball path will change, depending on the success of the shot. In 8 Ball, these shots leave the target object ball near the pocket. In 9 Ball, the miss will not leave an easy shot for your opponent.

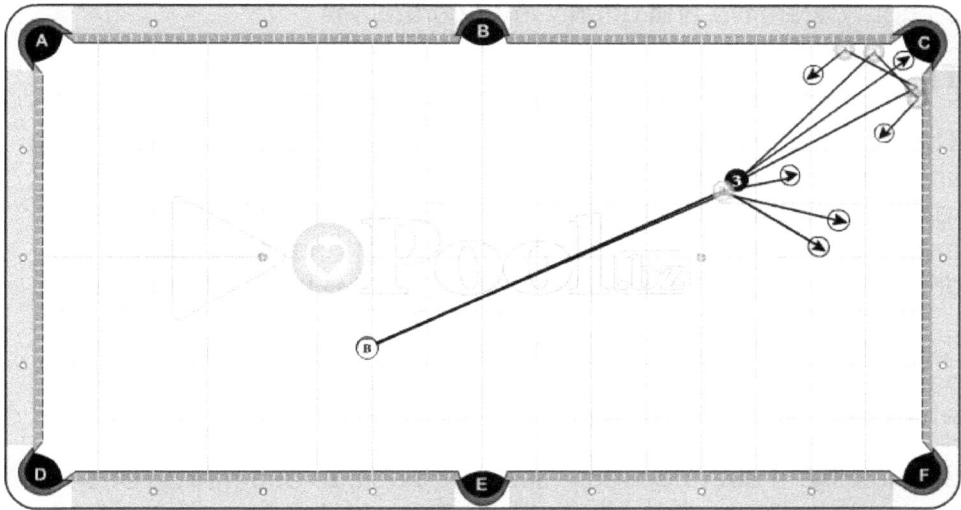

# Miscellaneous

This section covers a bunch of information that is useful for both defensive and offensive situations. This rounds out your education on both defensive and offensive opportunities.

## The "Ownership" Test

The question occasionally comes up – how do you know when you know a particular shot so well that you own it? Usually, the self-recognition doesn't occur until long after you actually have mastered the shot. It is a sudden realization that a previously difficult shot is now easy. This fact can take a long time to realize.

It's a lot more fun to understand that you really have mastered a particular shot. The test is surprisingly simple – you own a shot when you can shoot it with your eyes closed.

Sounds like a strange idea – like being able to use martial arts against an attack while blindfolded. Actually, the technique is not that difficult to apply. Here is the practice table procedure:

1. Set up the cue ball and object ball for the particular shot. Use donuts to mark the ball positions so can you repeat the shot.

2. While standing, determine what you will do (cue ball speed, spin and angle).

3. Get down on the shot and position your body for the stroke (including practice strokes).

4. Before executing the shot, close your eyes, pause for a moment, draw the cue stick back and make the stroke.

5. Freeze your position after the stroke (don't get up) and observe the results.

6. If you made the object ball and the cue ball did what you intended, repeat two more times. You really own the shot when you are successful three times in a row..

7. If you missed, do four consecutive successful shots with your eyes open, and then try with your eyes closed.

When one shot is owned, set up another shot with a change, for example a longer distance, different angle, or final cue ball position.

You might find yourself being more successful with an eyes-closed shot then eyes-open. Practice regularly and when you think you've got a newly mastered shot down, use this eyes-closed test.

## How to Escape a Hidden Ball Safety Against You

Just as you enjoy giving your opponent tough shots (especially hidden balls), it will also happen to you (accidentally or on purpose). If you know a few simple basics, you can constantly make legal shots. This can frustrate your opponent. As the match progresses, he will become less and less confident that any of his hidden ball safeties are going to be worth trying. Encourage this respect, since he won't know how simple it is.

When kicking, your target is really 6-3/4 inches wide, the width of three balls placed side by side. You don't have to contact the target object ball straight on to make a legal hit. Even the slightest graze is enough. Just make sure there is enough energy to get a ball to a rail or pocket.

*True Target Ball Width examples*

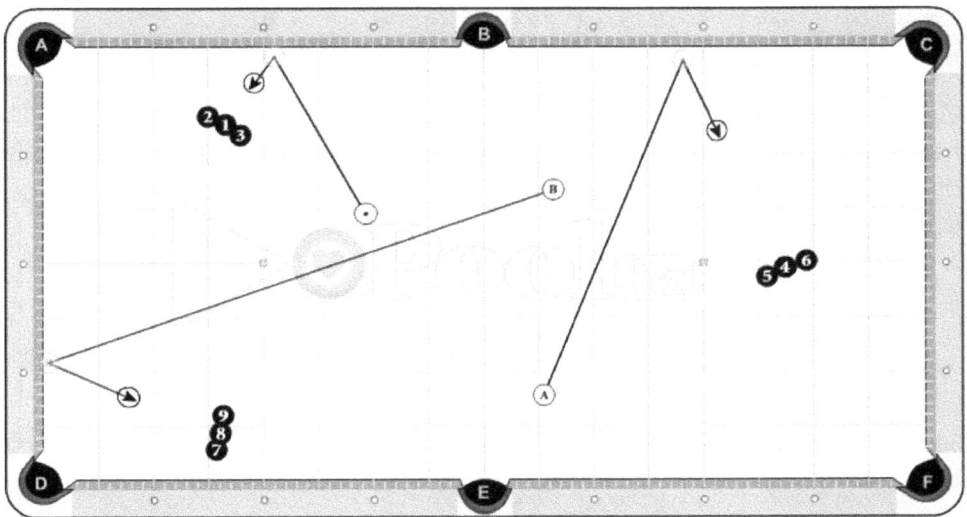

## How to Calculate One Cushion Kicks

When the cue ball and target object ball are about the same distance from the rail, the kicking calculation is the very simple "divide-by-2" (also known as "divide-in-half").

Draw a line from each ball straight to the rail. Measure the distance and divide that distance in half. The half-way point on the rail is the target for your cue ball.

*Divide-in-half (divide-by-2) examples*

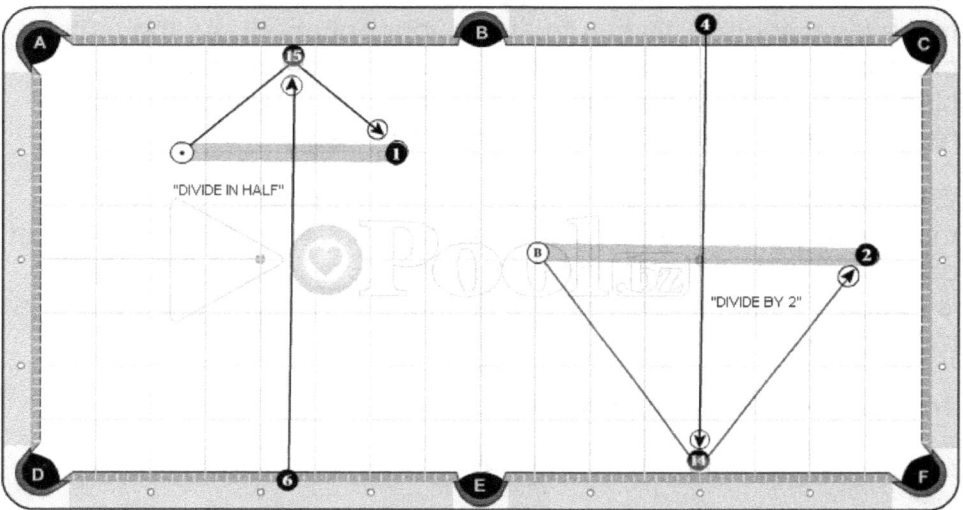

When the object ball is near a rail, you can use an easy "ghost ball" measurement technique. Measure the distance from the object ball directly to the cushion. Measure an equal distance from the edge of the cushion to a position off the table. Shoot at the "ghost ball".

## "Ghost ball" Measurement examples
Shoot straight at the ghost ball

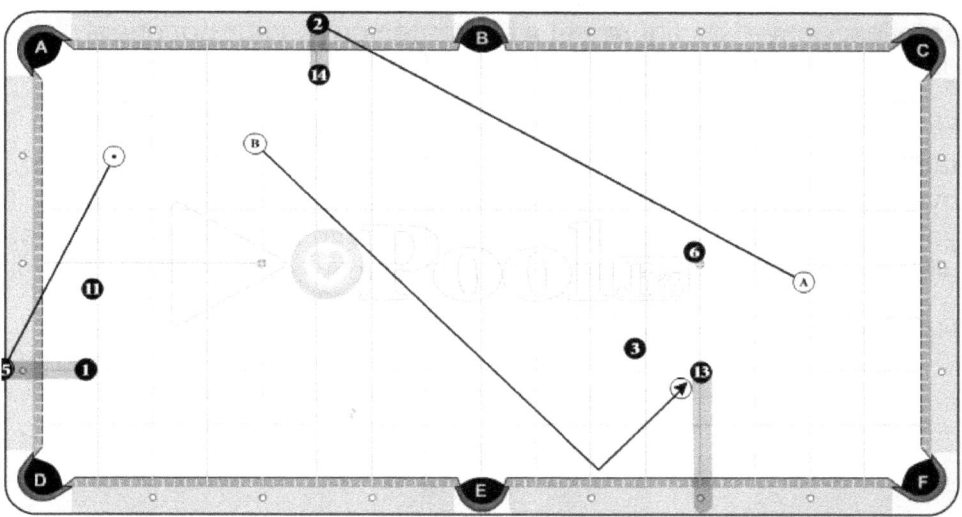

## How to Make Two Cushion Kicks

Sometimes it is easier to use a two-cushion kick to get to a hidden object ball. When the object ball is close to the cushion, the target is actually twice as big. You can hit the object ball directly (in a one-cushion kick) or come in off the rail (two-cushion kick). Use enough speed to make a legal hit.

### Object ball close to cushion - two-rail examples

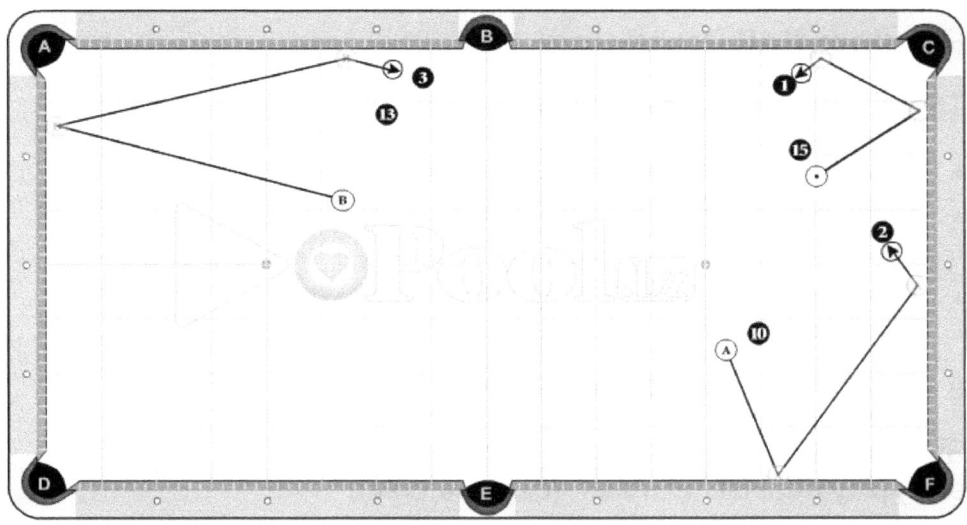

## A Recommended Basic Practice Routine

Safeties have to be practiced. You have to learn how to set up safeties, as well as figure out what to do you're your opponent (intentionally or by accident) leave you a limited table layout.

Have a basic routine ensures that when you get to the practice table, you use the time wisely. It's a waste of your time to practice by playing several racks by yourself. If you really want to improve your skills, you have to actually practice those skills. Otherwise, you will spend years of your life being a so-so player.

Here is a basic regimen:

1. 5 minutes – dial in your cue ball speed control.
2. 5 minutes – practice pocketing balls.
3. 5 minutes – practice pocketing and getting shape on a second ball.
4. 10 minutes – set up safety shots, and get into a safety battle.
5. Whatever else you need to practice on – shots missed in the last match, shots that you want to improve your pocketing or positioning skills.
6. End it with offensive/defensive 8 Ball or 9 Ball games, Chase game, etc.

## Random Ball Practicing

Throw some balls out on the table and work on these shots:

- Two-way shots (with and without intentional missing).
- Different ways to play individual and combination safeties with the same shot.
- Precision cue ball and object ball control. Put a piece of paper on the table where you want the cue ball or object ball to stop.

## 8 Ball Offense-Defense Game

Standard 8 Ball rules apply. Play against yourself. "You" (offense only) play against "Yourself" (defense only).

Set up the balls and break normally. When "you" shoot, play offense only. When you miss, your opponent "yourself" takes over.

"Yourself" can pocket balls, but is primarily defensive.

The game is played for 10 innings (or other set of innings). "You" win if you can complete the game before the inning set counts down. Otherwise, "yourself" is the winner.

This game teaches you how to recognize opportunities that can limit or otherwise restrict your opponent from winning the game.

## 9 Ball Offense-Defense Game

Standard 9 Ball rules apply. "You" (offense only) play against "Yourself" (defense only).

Set up the balls and break normally. When "you" shoot, you are trying to pocket balls and win the game. When you miss, your opponent "yourself" takes over.

"Yourself" can pocket balls, but is primarily defensive. At any time, "yourself" sees the opportunity to play defensively, do so.

The game is played for 10 innings (or other set of innings). "You" win if you can complete the game before the inning set counts down. Otherwise, "yourself" is the winner.

This game teaches you how to recognize opportunities that can limit or otherwise restrict your opponent from winning the game.

## Chase - a Game to Learn Kicking Skills

Copyright 2007 Allan P. Sand

This game teaches you how to kick to a target ball using angles and spins. These rules are for one player. The two player game could be played with each person playing a set, or (each player taking one of the balls as the cue ball) taking turns shot after shot.

### *Playing*

Each shot uses the same cue ball. Place a solid (1-8) on the head spot, a stripe (9-15) on the foot spot.

The shooter must call and hit one or more cushions and contact the other ball. To be a legal hit, after the ball contact, a ball must contact the cushion or be pocketed.

After each shot, the other ball becomes the cue ball. If a ball is pocketed, there is no foul. Spot the ball and continue play.

When you improve your one-rail kicks, practice two-rail kicks. For very good players, specify three-rail kicks. (This can also be a handicap if two players are competing.)

Luck cannot be counted. You must specify the number of rails and which rails.

### Scoring

Ten consecutive shots equal one inning. Ten innings equals one game. Points from all 10 frames are added for the final score.

*Variation:* 5 shots to an inning, 5 innings to a game,

One point is scored for each good hit.

If a foul, that stroke cannot score a point. All strokes (legal or not) count as one shot.

www.ingramcontent.com/pod-product-compliance
Lightning Source LLC
LaVergne TN
LVHW061217060426
835507LV00016B/1977